CORDELIA LYNN

Cordelia Lynn is a playwright, librettist and dramaturg. She received the Berwin Lee Award, 2020, the Harold Pinter Award, 2017 and the Jerwood New Playwright, 2015. Her opera with composer Sivan Eldar, *Like Flesh*, won the Fedora Opera Prize, 2021. Her piece with composer Laura Bowler, *Houses Slide*, was nominated for an Ivor Award, 2022. Cordelia is a MacDowell Fellow.

Plays include *Sea Creatures* (Hampstead Theatre); *Love and Other Acts of Violence* (Donmar Warehouse); *fragments* (short, Young Vic), *Hedda Tesman*, adapt. Henrik Ibsen (Headlong Theatre/Chichester Festival Theatre/Lowry, Manchester); *Three Sisters*, adapt. Anton Chekhov (Almeida Theatre); *One for Sorrow*, *Lela & Co.* (Royal Court Theatre); *Confessions* (short, Theatre Uncut/Traverse, Edinburgh/Bristol Old Vic); *Best Served Cold* (VAULT Festival).

Opera includes *Like Flesh* (Operas Nationals de Lille/Montpellier/Lorraine); *Houses Slide* (Royal Festival Hall, Southbank Centre); *Miranda* (Opera Comique & European tour).

Dramaturgy includes *Henry V* (Headlong Theatre, Shakespeare's Globe and UK tour); *Lucia di Lammermoor* (Royal Opera House).

Cordelia Lynn

SEA CREATURES

NICK HERN BOOKS

London

www.nickhernbooks.co.uk

A Nick Hern Book

Sea Creatures first published in Great Britain as a paperback original in 2023 by Nick Hern Books Limited, The Glasshouse, 49a Goldhawk Road, London W12 8QP

Sea Creatures copyright © 2023 Cordelia Lynn

Cover photography: Oliver Sjöström/Pexels

Designed and typeset by Nick Hern Books, London
Printed in Great Britain by Mimeo Ltd, Huntingdon, Cambridgeshire PE29 6XX

A CIP catalogue record for this book is available from the British Library

ISBN 978 1 83904 214 0

Sea Creatures was first performed at Hampstead Theatre, London, on 24 March 2023, with the following cast:

SHIRLEY	Geraldine Alexander
GEORGE	Pearl Chanda
SARAH	Thusitha Jayasundera
MARK	Tom Mothersdale
TONI	Grace Saif
FRED THE FISHERMAN	Tony Turner
OLD WOMAN	June Watson
Director	James Macdonald
Designer	Zoë Hurwitz
Lighting	Jack Knowles
Sound	Max Pappenheim

Sea Creatures was written at MacDowell, for whose generosity I am very grateful.

C.L.

Characters

SHIRLEY, *late fifties*
SARAH, *early fifties, her partner*
GEORGIA/GEORGE, *around thirty, her daughter*
ROBIN, *mid-twenties, her daughter*
ANTONIA/TONI, *early twenties, her daughter*
MARK, *late twenties*
FRED THE FISHERMAN, *timeless*
OLD WOMAN, *very*

Scene

There is a cottage near the sea, which was built by a fisherman, so as to be close to the source of his livelihood. No fishermen live there now, and around half the year it stands empty. The cottage was built about a century ago but, over time, to account for family and modern convenience, rooms have been added and refurbishments made. The most recent addition is a new kitchen, with walls mostly of glass to look out onto the sea. Because of the glass the kitchen is filled with the weather and the day and the night as they make their exchange. This is where the play is set.

Scene changes should indicate, by way of light and weather, time passing. The characters should do and be seen to do what is necessary in terms of entering and exiting, bringing on/taking off/tidying up props. It is unlikely the action lasts less than a month, or more than two months.

Other Important

George is seven/eight months pregnant.

Toni is in her pyjamas.

Robin isn't there.

Bold indicates something imagined.

… on its own line indicates something unsaid.

/ indicates an interruption.

… as part of a line indicates a tailing off or in.

This text went to press before the end of rehearsals and so may differ slightly from the play as performed.

1. No One's Seen the Baby

Early morning.

SARAH *comes into the kitchen. Crocs, a swimming costume, a hoodie, goggles and a towel. She gets herself a glass of water and drinks it then leaves by the sea door.*

Time passes.

SHIRLEY *comes in by the sea door. She boils the kettle and while the kettle boils she takes a shell out of her pocket and puts it where the shells go and then prepares the cafetière. When the kettle is boiled she makes the coffee and takes it and a mug into the house.*

Time passes.

SHIRLEY (*meanwhile*). Stood on the shore last night and Robin came crawling out of the sea. The waves pulled back like a blanket and there was Robin. When the waves washed over her they lifted and carried her and then, reluctant, dragged her back. It was a slow crawling, and I didn't want her to crawl out. I didn't know what she was doing in the sea but it seemed to be the best place for her. When she was fast on the shore I saw that she didn't have any legs. She was making a huge effort to crawl out of the sea with just her arms. I saw the flesh and skin trailing from her waist, and rivulets of water run down her skin into the surf when the waves pulled back. I saw the peaks of every wave, every peak like whips of cream but black as blood. There was no blood. She paused for breath and looked up at me. She had not been coming for me and she was pleased to see me, but I was afraid... And I did not give her my hand...

GEORGE *comes into the kitchen. She boils the kettle and looks for the cafetière and can't find it. She slams the cupboard door then rolls a cigarette. When the kettle is boiled she makes a mug of tea.*

SARAH *comes back from her swim through the sea door. She has a glass of water then puts her glass in the dishwasher.*

SARAH (*meanwhile*). Morning.

GEORGE. Shirley took the cafetière again.

SARAH. Oh...

GEORGE. There are more of us than there are of her.

SARAH. We'll get another one.

GEORGE. Was it cold?

SARAH. Not too cold.

GEORGE. There's going to be a heatwave.

SARAH. I saw.

SARAH *goes into the house. When the tea is ready* GEORGE *takes her tea and her cigarette outside and sits at the garden table and smokes her cigarette and drinks her tea.*

Time passes.

TONI *comes in from the house and makes toast then looks for the cafetière.* GEORGE *comes back in by the sea door.*

GEORGE. Don't bother. Shirley took it.

TONI. Oh.

TONI *makes a mug of tea.*

GEORGE. Every morning she takes the cafetière

TONI. She needs it

GEORGE. There's only one of her and three of us

TONI. But she needs it to work

GEORGE. It isn't democratic.

TONI. Have we had this conversation before?

GEORGE. I don't know.

TONI. I think we have but it's hard to tell

GEORGE. Sarah says we'll get another one.

TONI. Has she said that before too? (*Pause.*) I woke up crying this morning. Do you ever do that? Wake up / crying

GEORGE (*to the baby*). Fuck off!

TONI. Is she kicking?

GEORGE. Always kicking. Kicking or poking or twisting around, backflips and somersaults, break-dancing, figure skating...

TONI *goes and puts her hand on* GEORGE*'s belly.*

TONI. Hello tiny acrobat... (*Laughs.*) She'll be a trapeze artist. She'll run away with a circus. She'll wear a glittery white costume and fly like a gull

GEORGE. I hate gulls

TONI. Like a tern. Everyone will cheer and applaud her...

GEORGE *lights a cigarette.*

I love the smell. It smells like you. Will the baby smell like you / too

GEORGE. Don't.

Pause.

TONI. One... two... three... four... Four days left until Robin and Mark come.

GEORGE. If she comes.

TONI. Mark will bring her.

SARAH *comes in from the house, dressed, hair damp. She makes toast and tea.*

SARAH. Morning.

TONI. Did you swim?

SARAH. Oh yes.

TONI. Was it cold?

SARAH. Not so cold.

TONI. There's going to be a heatwave.

SARAH. I saw.

TONI. Do you remember years ago there was a heatwave and all the grass burnt black? Like a volcano had swept through and only spared the house.

SARAH. That must have been before my time

GEORGE. It was

SARAH. I don't remember black grass

TONI. I think if there was a volcano it would probably spare the house

GEORGE. Or Grandpa would go and shout at it

TONI. 'You volcano! You with your ash and your lava! I'll teach you a lesson you'll never forget!'

GEORGE. And then go and sit in the shed in the dark with the spiders and cry.

TONI. I like spiders. They know how to stay still.

SARAH. It's not a shed any more. It's a lovely studio with no spiders and no dark.

TONI. When you turned the shed into a studio you let the light in...

   SARAH *kisses the top of her head.*

   It's true.

SARAH. What do you want for dinner?

GEORGE. A miscarriage.

SARAH. The courgettes are in flower. We can fry the flowers in salt and pepper and a tiny bit of chilli and sit outside.

TONI. Can we drink the champagne?

SARAH. No.

TONI. I like champagne because it's like a biscuit but it makes you drunk.

SARAH. We can have it on Robin and Mark's first evening.

TONI. Sarah and I are going to meet them at the station. Do you want to come?

GEORGE. No.

TONI. Robin hasn't seen the baby / yet

GEORGE. No one's seen the baby.

Pause.

SARAH. Are you sad today?

GEORGE. …

SARAH. Have you had breakfast? Would you like eggs? I'll make them however you want

TONI. Like in America /

GEORGE *runs out of the room.*

Pause.

SARAH. Would you like eggs?

TONI. How's the painting?

SARAH. It gets bigger.

TONI. Is it deep yet?

SARAH. Not yet.

TONI. You can't get lost in it?

SARAH. Not yet.

TONI. When you get lost how do you find your way back?

What do you navigate by? Is there a map?

SARAH. What are you going to do today?

TONI *(after some thought)*. Practise staying still.

SARAH. Like a spider?

TONI. Like a spider.

SARAH (*going out by the sea door with her tea*). Maybe you can start being a spider when you're washed and dressed...

    TONI *practises staying still.*

    Time passes.

    Out at sea the bells ring.

TONI (*eventually*). She'll be a witch. She'll be beautiful and cold and she'll put her heart in an egg for safe keeping and live for a thousand years. Music will call to her and grain will be bartered with her and she'll ask for your firstborn child and when the time comes she won't be tricked. But a man who knows his true worth will appear, and he'll find the egg and take it in his hard hands...

2. Where's Robin?

Night. Moonlight.

SHIRLEY *in a jacket at the sea door. She has just come in.*
MARK *in the kitchen. They look at each other.*

MARK. She's not here...

    Pause.

SHIRLEY. How long?

MARK. A week.

SHIRLEY. Not too long then...

MARK. I used to call the police. I stopped calling the police. It was embarrassing when she always turned up.

SHIRLEY. That's how it happens.

MARK. She does come back. Always eventually comes /

SHIRLEY. Until she doesn't.

MARK. ...

TONI *runs in and stops*.

SHIRLEY. Toni... Yes. Good...

SHIRLEY *goes into the house*.

TONI. You're here.

MARK. Yes.

TONI. Where's Robin?

MARK. I don't know.

TONI. Oh.

How long?

MARK. A week.

TONI. Not so long then...

MARK. No.

TONI. You look different.

MARK. Do I?

TONI. You look older.

MARK. I am older.

TONI. And you're a day early. I was counting down... Sarah and I were going to meet you at the station in the car. How did you get here?

MARK. I walked.

TONI. Walked!

How did you know where we were?

MARK. I didn't. I got lost. I walked for five hours. It was so hot and I had no water

TONI. There's a heatwave

MARK. I felt faint but I kept walking. Then it got dark...

I thought maybe she was here already, that she left without me...

TONI. And we thought she was with you...

MARK *spreads his arms, then lets them drop.*

George is having a baby. I'm going to be an aunt. But don't tell her.

MARK (*'tell'*). Who?

TONI. George.

Beat.

MARK. I knew your house by a sense of homecoming. It washed over me as I passed below on the beach and I followed the track up. There was a lantern lit on the gate like an eye, and I opened the gate and walked in.

TONI. A lantern?

MARK. An old hurricane lamp.

TONI. ...Did anything happen? When you walked in.

MARK. No.

TONI. ...

MARK. You shouldn't leave your doors unlocked. At night.

Out at sea, a ship's horn. Long and mournful.

I thought your mum would be scary but she isn't. I was so shy about meeting her. I've read everything she's written. Her work forms the basis of my PhD though I come to different conclusions.

TONI. Robin might still come. We just have to wait. I'll show you your room, which is Robin's room. Where's your bag?

MARK *takes a toothbrush out of his back trouser pocket and holds it up.*

We were going to buy another cafetière when we picked you up. I guess we can go into town anyway and buy you some underwear too.

GEORGE, *nightdress, comes in and stands in the doorway. She turns on the light. She and MARK look at each other.*

GEORGE. How long?

MARK. A week.

(*The baby.*) Congratulations /

GEORGE *runs out.*

TONI. I'll show you the important things… That's where the shells go. If you find a compelling shell and want to take it out of its natural habitat you can put it there with the other shells. You can also put compelling pebbles there and bits of skeleton. Cuttlefish go in the garden. That's the sea door. It's how you get to the sea. The studio's at the bottom of the garden which is where Sarah paints and sometimes sleeps if she doesn't want to sleep with Shirley which is mostly now because Shirley is a demanding sleeper. You can't go into the studio without her invitation and you can't go into Shirley's study without *her* invitation so even though those are important things I won't be able to show you now. This way…

She goes into the house, turning the light off as she passes. MARK *scratches his head.*

(*Off.*) This way!

3. Paper Sailing Boats

Late afternoon.

TONI *has been admiring the new cafetière.*

TONI. She'll be a coffee farmer. She'll live in Panama with a wide-brimmed hat and she'll walk through the plantation and know the health of her plants just by looking. She'll know the worth of the ground beneath her feet. She'll know the weather, how it's written in the sky. At harvest time she'll run the lovely beans through her fingers and know the weight and the shape of them /

MARK *comes in through the sea door with scissors and herbs.*

MARK. Who are you talking to?

TONI. I wasn't talking. What are you doing?

MARK. Gathering herbs.

TONI. Why?

MARK. I'm going to make moules marinière.

TONI. What did Sarah say about you cooking?

MARK. I didn't ask.

TONI. Sarah usually cooks. Except Sundays when Shirley cooks.

MARK *lays out and prepares the herbs on the work surface.*

MARK. She said she bought mussels.

TONI. In the sink. How did you know what to pick?

MARK. Because of the recipe.

TONI *(going over, interested)*. I don't know what things are...

MARK. That's disgusting. I didn't have a garden. I didn't even have window boxes. I just had concrete and misery.

TONI. I like concrete

MARK. If I'd had a garden like this I'd know every flower and shrub.

TONI. Shirley knows things too but she pretends not to so people will leave her alone.

MARK. Why do you call your mum Shirley?

TONI *(after some thought)*. It's her name.

MARK. I think it's weird when people call their parents by their names.

TONI. You can call her Mum if you prefer. I don't think she'd mind

MARK. I don't want to call her Mum

TONI. She doesn't really distinguish between things

MARK. I've got my own mum

TONI. Do you?

Beat.

MARK. How old are you?

TONI. Twenty-two.

MARK. Twenty-two!

TONI. …

MARK. Are you at university?

TONI. …

MARK. Have you graduated?

TONI. …

MARK. Did you go to your mother's university? Did she get you a place? Was it easy for you?

TONI. …

MARK. What do you do?

TONI *demonstrates staying still but* MARK *doesn't notice because she just stays still.*

Well you're an adult. You should start behaving normally and you should know things. Here… (*Thrusts parsley in her face.*) What's this.

TONI. Par-sley…

MARK. Flat-leaf parsley. (*Thrusts sage in her face.*) And this?

TONI. Um

MARK. Sage. Smell it. You smelling it?

TONI. Yes

MARK. Remember it. Good with pork and if you fry it in butter you can make sage butter. These are dried bay leaves. See how they break apart in your hand? Stocks and soups and stews need bay leaves. What's this?

TONI. Lavender

MARK. Rosemary! Smell it.

TONI. I don't want to

MARK. Roast meats, especially lamb and beef. See how you can strip the needles from the stem. What's this?

TONI. Don't

MARK. Look at it /

GEORGE *comes in.*

GEORGE. What are you doing?

MARK. Cooking.

GEORGE. Sarah cooks. Except on /

MARK. Now I'm cooking.

(*The baby.*) How many months?

GEORGE *runs out of the room.*

TONI. I told you not to remind her.

MARK. What's wrong with her?

TONI. She's trapped.

MARK. Where's the father?

TONI. Nobody knows, nobody cares...

MARK. That's just irresponsible.

TONI. I was really looking forward to you coming. It's been two years since we met and I liked you so much. We sat by the canal and it was warm and sunny and Robin seemed calm like I hadn't seen her for years. You went away for half an hour and I began to worry you wouldn't come back but then you did with a punnet of strawberries. We ate them all with our legs dangling over the side of the canal. You were so nice to her and you were also nice to me and I actually had a little crush on you because at that age I still confused liking shyly with desire. I thought about you and Robin a lot. I imagined all sorts of good things for you. You were so gentle. You don't seem gentle any more...

Pause.

MARK. Why do you like concrete?

TONI. When you look at it you can see all the vines and roots growing over and people will say 'these were once temples or palaces' but actually they were just… car parks. Council blocks. Coach stations

MARK. Thyme. (*The herb*.) It's thyme. In the spring it has little purple flowers. Like stars.

SHIRLEY comes in from the house.

SHIRLEY. Mussels. Delicious.

She leaves by the sea door.

MARK. Where is she going?

TONI. Shirley walks on the beach three times a day. Once in the morning before she starts work, once again when she finishes work and once at night to keep the dreams away for a little while longer.

MARK. I have to admit that I had an ulterior motive in convincing Robin to come home for the summer. I was hoping Shirley would read and comment on my PhD.

TONI. If you come to different conclusions won't she just comment that you're wrong?

MARK. Or maybe she'll recognise my argument as superior and everything I've worked so hard for will be validated.

TONI. Shirley is good at Sunday lunch and finding shells and being the youngest woman to receive a professorship in the history of the university but she isn't good at validating.

MARK. …

TONI. If you don't adjust your expectations you'll be sad.

MARK. You can help me cook if you like.

TONI. I don't know how.

MARK. I'll show you.

He gets the potatoes and rinses them in a colander and puts them on the work surface and takes a knife from the knife block. He gets a pan and puts it by the colander. He gets a

*bowl and an egg and a whisk and keeps the egg and the
whisk in the bowl and sets it aside.*

TONI (*meanwhile*). How do you know where the things are?

MARK. I have an instinct for other people's houses

TONI. I don't know where the things are

MARK. It's a general rule that things have their places and in a
kitchen most people abide by that rule

TONI. Except for the cafetière because it's never there which is
how I know where it is

> SARAH *appears in the glass behind them and peers in. After
> a while she goes away again.*

MARK. We're going to make chips to go with the mussels and
mayonnaise to go with the chips

TONI. Like in Belgium!

MARK. Mayonnaise is actually a simple sauce, it just takes
time and physical effort if you don't use an electric whisk
which I don't

TONI. I've never been to Belgium

MARK. I do as much as is reasonable with my own body
because I believe in a physical association with your actions
in the world

TONI. I've never been anywhere really

MARK. I whisk my own mayonnaise and I knead my own
bread and once I made thirty-two meringues whisking the
egg whites manually

TONI. Fred the fisherman says there's a city in Belgium
populated entirely by bureaucrats

MARK. My arm was in agony but –

'Fred the fisherman'?

TONI. He brings lobsters and tells stories.

MARK. ...

TONI. ...

MARK. ...

TONI. ...

MARK. I'm going to clean and debeard the mussels. You chop the potatoes. Chop them rough but thinly, no need to peel, and put them in that pan.

TONI chops the potatoes. She perhaps manages to chop one potato. MARK knocks the barnacles off the mussels with a paring knife. When he has finished he starts debearding them.

(*Meanwhile.*) We're going to parboil and then roast them in a big tray in the oven with oil and the rosemary and lots of salt. The other herbs are for the bouquet garni. We'll tie parsley and bay leaves and thyme together with a short length of thread and steam the mussels with garlic, white wine and the herbs. In the south of France dried orange peel is included in the bouquet but we're not going to do that because it would be weird.

TONI. I've never been to France.

MARK. You're doing that stupidly. Let me show you.

He stands behind her and takes the knife and chops around her.

See?

TONI (*very still, with her eyes closed*). Yes.

MARK. Good.

He gives her back the knife and she carries on chopping as before.

It is not for me a question of saving time. Part of why I try and do as much as is reasonable with my own body is so that I can experience a realistic passage of time. I wash my clothes by hand, I walk everywhere in the city. If I have to wake up two hours earlier to get somewhere then that is what I do. When I came up here on the train I watched the landscape slide past the window as though on a television screen and I felt dizzy. Waves of panic washed over me until I walked them away when I walked from the station to this house.

GEORGE *comes in with a box and empties it on the table. It is a game of Jenga.*

…For me it is a question of being good at things, or at least competent. You're bad at chopping potatoes. How do you sleep at night?

They prepare the food. GEORGE *plays Jenga.*

How many have you chopped?

TONI. Two including the half that you chopped.

MARK. You debeard the mussels and I'll chop the potatoes. Normally you can just rip the beard out with your fingers, but if it won't come cut it with the paring knife. If you come across an open mussel, discard it. Once they're cooked the / reverse

TONI. Ow!

MARK. What's wrong?

TONI. I cut myself…

MARK. Let me see…

TONI *gives him her hand.*

It's not so deep. **Here…**

TONI. What are you doing?

MARK. The salt will clean it

TONI. No don't – !

He forces her hand into the salt dish. She screams.

Ow!

MARK. What's wrong?

TONI. I cut myself…

MARK. Let me see…

TONI *gives him her hand.*

It's not so deep. Do you want a plaster?

TONI. I don't like plasters.

MARK. That's enough cooking for you. You should go and get washed and dressed before dinner.

TONI. I don't like getting dressed

MARK (*clapping his hands at her*). Go and get dressed!

TONI *runs out.*

Pause. MARK *carries on chopping the potatoes.*

GEORGE (*focusing on the Jenga*). You should be nice to Toni.

MARK. I am nice to Toni. It's absurd for her to wear her pyjamas all the time.

GEORGE. 'Absurd.' (*Laughs.*)

MARK. I don't think I've seen her out of them since I've been here. It's dangerous.

GEORGE. The sea is more dangerous but you're not worrying about the sea.

MARK. She won't distinguish between night and day properly if she wears her pyjamas all the time.

GEORGE. It's Shirley who doesn't distinguish between things

MARK. Depression runs in your family. You should all take more responsibility.

GEORGE (*laughs*).

MARK. Does she have a learning difficulty?

GEORGE. 'Learning difficulty.' (*Laughs.*)

MARK. She acts like a child

GEORGE. She has a child's idea of justice

MARK. And you all encourage her

GEORGE. Neat, pure, catastrophic…

MARK *chops,* GEORGE *plays.*

(*Eventually.*) Did Robin ever tell you the story of how Shirley became deaf in one ear?

MARK. …

GEORGE. After the last sperm bank left and before Sarah came, Shirley was on her own with us. Shirley was already engaged in being a genius, but it's difficult being a genius if you're a woman with three children and no money, and because of the nature of Shirley's genius she had very little money... One night she came back home after lecturing all day and she had left us all alone all day on a rainy day and Robin had got it into her head that the best thing for the notes Shirley had been taking for her next work of towering genius was for the pages to be folded into sailing boats and sailed down the gutter. Which seems perfectly reasonable from a seven-year-old's perspective but from the perspective of an adult genius was just an act of barbaric vandalism. So Shirley took Robin by her little arm and screamed at her. But when she had finished the screaming didn't stop in Robin's head. The screaming went on all night and all of the next day and into the next night and she told me and Toni, 'I can hear the bells, I can smell the sea, the water's at my feet the water's at my ankles the water's at my knees...' Being an intelligent child, Toni understood that by screaming at her for so long, Shirley had scared Robin's soul right out of her body, and that soul had hitched a ride on one of those paper sailing boats, fled down the gutter into the sewage system, and sailed all the way out to sea where it had taken shelter in the drowned village just up the coast from where we are. Robin could hear the submerged church bells ringing, and she would hear them ringing forever more... So late one night when Shirley was asleep, Toni took a sewing needle, and she crept into Shirley's room

MARK. No

GEORGE. And she jammed that needle right into Shirley's left ear canal

MARK. Fuck off

GEORGE. Neat. Pure. Catastrophic

MARK. I don't believe you

GEORGE. You should be nice to Toni

MARK. Robin has tinnitus triggered by stress

GEORGE. You should be nice to Toni.

4. Sea Burial

Morning.

SARAH *and* TONI *eating toast and drinking coffee.* SARAH *in her swimming gear, but dry.*

TONI. I was really looking forward to seeing him again but now he's here he's strange and cold.

SARAH. He misses Robin.

TONI. We've been missing Robin for longer than he has and we're not cold.

SARAH. George is a little cold... And he's not as used to what Robin does to you as we are.

TONI. But he's always *doing* things.

SARAH. Some people like to do things

TONI. Yesterday he tried to teach me how to iron a shirt.

SARAH (*laughs*).

TONI. He said, 'It's absurd not to know how to iron a shirt. Everyone should know how to iron a shirt.' He stood me between him and the ironing board. I could feel the heat from the iron and had to stay very still and he said 'See? See? See?' and I said 'Yes yes yes' but he didn't know I had my eyes closed.

SARAH. Good girl.

TONI. Why do people want flat clothes?

MARK *comes in from the house with gardening gloves. He stops in the room and wants to say something but then goes out by the sea door.*

SARAH. I think he's trying to be nice.

TONI. But it isn't nice

SARAH. Like a big brother

TONI. It hurts.

Beat.

SARAH (*careful*). He hurt you?

TONI. No.

Beat.

SARAH. It's important, sometimes, to distinguish between the real, and the felt, and the feared.

TONI. It's his fault. He came in unannounced. At night. He came up from the sea... He said there was a lantern on the gate

SARAH. A lantern?

A loud crack. They go still.

Pause.

It's gone.

They settle.

TONI. How's the painting?

SARAH. Wading out...

TONI. You're still by the shore?

SARAH. Oh yes. Sand between my toes...

SHIRLEY *passes outside the windows, back from her walk. She stops and stares at the ground, then she crouches down and stays down.*

TONI. Maybe the baby will be a painter like you.

SARAH. Maybe...

TONI. She'll stretch her own canvas and cut her own mounts and frames. She'll know the true application of colour and shape will reveal its meaning to her. She'll give her entire life just so that one day, when she's very old, she'll be able to say that she understands her medium.

SARAH. You know... When the baby comes things are going to change.

TONI. There'll be a baby.

SHIRLEY *stands again and carries on past.*

SARAH. Sentences are going to remain unfinished, there'll be a concentration of attention. You have to prepare yourself...

SHIRLEY *comes in by the sea door.*

SHIRLEY. You didn't go for your swim...

SARAH. We were discussing Mark.

SHIRLEY. Who?

Oh yes. The angry man.

TONI. He keeps doing things in a deliberate sort of way.

SHIRLEY. There's a dead bird on the decking.

TONI. Oh no...

SHIRLEY. A swallow. With a bead of blood held in its beak...

TONI. We should bury it.

SHIRLEY. A sea burial.

SARAH. I'll take it with me when I swim.

TONI. Take it far out...

SARAH. How was your walk?

SHIRLEY. Unsettling. It's still early but already so hot. The grasses and dunes were waves and I lost sight of where I was between the land and the sea. When I made the head I looked out and there were dozens of seals

SARAH. Seals?

SHIRLEY. Bobbing in the water, eyes and whiskers above the water line. Very still and waiting... What do you think they wanted from me?

SARAH (*gentle*). I don't think they were there Shirley

SHIRLEY. They watched me as I walked away... Like very sad children

SARAH. That was in Ireland. Do you remember in Ireland, five years ago?

SHIRLEY. ...

TONI. It's true Shirley, you and Sarah did go to Ireland five years ago

   MARK *walks past the windows, stops, bends down and stands again. Carries on walking past.*

SARAH. We walked to a bay and when we looked out over the water there were dozens of seals. Do you remember that that was then and today is now?

   Beat.

SHIRLEY. Five years ran to sand beneath my feet...

SARAH. You're back now

   MARK *comes in by the sea door. He holds his gloved hand out.*

MARK. I found this dead bird on the decking. I know it's not attractive but if this has happened before you might want to consider getting stickers on the glass.

   They stare at the dead bird he has brought into the house.

TONI. Disaster.

5. An Instinct for Ginger

Early evening.

MARK *and* SHIRLEY. SHIRLEY *is just going for her walk.*

MARK. I would like to speak to you about something.

SHIRLEY. ...

MARK. ...

SHIRLEY. ...

MARK. This morning when I came out of my bedroom / there

SHIRLEY. Robin's bedroom.

Beat.

MARK. This morning when I came out of Robin's bedroom
there was a trail of sand...

SHIRLEY. ...

MARK. It began in the corridor at the wall, roughly where
Robin's bedroom stops and becomes Toni's, and it drew
round the door of Robin's bedroom in a curved line to the
wall of the house.

SHIRLEY. ...

MARK. I went outside and the trail of sand began again on the
ground at the wall where it had left off, drew round the
corner of the house, beneath my windows and stopped at the
wall again below Toni's room.

SHIRLEY. ...

MARK. I went back inside, into Toni's room, and just where the
wall separates her and Robin's room the sand continued till it
met the wall between her room and the corridor, finally
joining up with itself in the corridor on the other side.

SHIRLEY. ...

Around here, TONI *appears in the windows and peers in.
Whenever she senses they might turn and see her, she ducks
out of sight, then slowly creeps up again and watches.*

MARK. What I am trying to say is that, with no respect paid to structural boundaries, someone has enclosed my room in a circle of sand

SHIRLEY. Robin's room

MARK. This seems to me not only potentially unhygienic but also disturbed.

SHIRLEY. …

MARK. I am discomforted by having the room I am sleeping in encircled with sand in the night.

SHIRLEY. …

MARK. What I would like, as I have not seen Toni all day and suspect she is hiding from me, is for you to tell your daughter to clean up the sand, and to cease and desist from such childish / behaviour

SHIRLEY. That would only encourage her.

MARK. …

SHIRLEY. She's just trying to protect you.

MARK. …

SHIRLEY. Or maybe she's trying to protect us…

Beat.

SHIRLEY *goes to leave by the sea door.*

MARK. I left my PhD on your desk!

She stops.

SHIRLEY. So that's what that was… I saw the title and couldn't remember having written it…

MARK. I was hoping you'd read it.

SHIRLEY. …

MARK. It would mean everything to / me.

SHIRLEY. You came into my study without my invitation.

MARK. …

SHIRLEY. You move like a cat, on quiet feet, so we never know where you're going to appear next... But really you're a bull in a china shop. Panicked and breaking everything. The more you thrash about the more you'll get hurt.

She's gone. MARK *stands.*

SARAH (*off*). Don't be long, dinner will be ready soon...

SARAH *comes in by the sea door and stops.* MARK *just stands.*

Oh, hello. I was about to get started on the dinner...

MARK *takes a skewer from a jar of utensils on the kitchen counter and methodically and quickly stabs himself four times in the cheek.*

Don't be long, dinner will be ready soon...

SARAH *comes in by the sea door and stops.*

Oh, hello. I was about to get started on the dinner...

MARK. Let me help

SARAH. There's really no need

MARK. I'm happy to help

SARAH. I'm used to doing it all myself

MARK. Which I think is wrong. Your daughters should /

SARAH. They're not my daughters.

I love them, but I came later.

MARK. Whose?

SARAH. Just Shirley's.

MARK. Where are the fathers?

SARAH. Nobody knows, nobody cares...

Did Robin really tell you so little?

Beat.

MARK. If you had help you'd be able to focus more on your art...

SARAH. You're so thoughtful, but it really isn't necessary

They go about the room, gathering, in a carefully calibrated dance that avoids bumping into each other or reaching for the same food item/utensil, without appearing to do so. GEORGE *has joined* TONI *at the window, watching and ducking out of sight.*

MARK. No I insist

SARAH. Especially today, it's so hot, we don't need much

MARK. A salad of sorts, fresh and cold...

SARAH. Baby gem lettuce, radishes, dill

MARK. Green tomatoes to sweeten it

SARAH. I would keep those separate, sliced into discs with lots of salt and olive oil

MARK. And we have to eat the bream

SARAH. Oh no, I think even a bream will be too much in this weather

MARK. No need to cook it. We can chop it into small pieces and marinate it in lemon till the flesh turns milky, with tiny cubes of peach folded in.

Really, it's delicious.

SARAH. ...That does sound good...

MARK *puts his hand on* SARAH*'s hand, which she has reached for a knife.* TONI *and* GEORGE *still watching at the window.*

MARK. I'm so grateful to be here. It would mean the world to me if you'd let me help...

SARAH. And this is how you'd like to spend your summer is it?

MARK (*taking the knife from under her hand*). Yes, exactly

SARAH. Just be here and / cook...

MARK. Wait for Robin... (*Pause.*) Ginger as well, I think. Though I'm not sure how yet, I have an instinct for ginger.

6. A Sadness Like That

Afternoon. Astonishingly hot.

FRED THE FISHERMAN, GEORGE *and* TONI *at the table, drinking tea,* GEORGE *rolling cigarettes. There are two lobsters on the table. Every now and again one of the lobsters optimistically makes a break for it, and* FRED *casually pulls it back.* MARK *is at the counter, chopping.*

Pause.

FRED. There's a storm coming.

MARK. …

GEORGE. They've said there'll be a storm for weeks now

FRED. They have and they're wrong. But I'm never wrong about storms.

MARK. Predicting the weather is an imprecise science

GEORGE. It's like living in a light bulb…

MARK. Predicting the weather /

FRED. It'll break

MARK. Is an imprecise / science

FRED. And what exactly is a precise science?

MARK (*momentarily flummoxed*). …

FRED. Eh?

GEORGE. Loving…

MARK (*grateful*). Loving is not a science.

GEORGE. You speculate. Experiment. Trial and error. And then at the end of it all you draw your conclusions. (*Lights two cigarettes at once and gives one to* FRED.)

FRED. She's got you there son.

MARK. Loving is not precise. If there's one thing that can be said for loving it's that it's /

TONI. Oh!

MARK. Messy...

TONI (*the pessimistic lobster*). What is it doing! All those bubbles round its mouth?

FRED. That's the air escaping.

TONI. You mean it's screaming?

Beat.

FRED. No need to think of it like that...

TONI. Look at it gathering there, like foam...

GEORGE. Look at it waving its legs...

They watch the lobster. MARK *chops.*

TONI. Poor lobster...

MARK. Don't sympathise with your food.

FRED. If you want to be kind you'll freeze it. Puts 'em in a coma before you boil 'em.

TONI. Sarah has to paint one first.

FRED. Does she now

TONI. Sarah used to paint other things but when the menopause came she found she could only paint lobsters. Even when she does a self-portrait she paints a lobster. She used to do portraits of other people too but after the lobsters they said they couldn't see a likeness.

FRED. I'd have my money back.

TONI. People did. Except for one man who really did look like a lobster. A cooked lobster. He was all red in the face and had these whiskers...

GEORGE. He was more like a walrus

TONI. He thought it was funny

GEORGE. A sunburnt walrus

TONI. He hung the portrait in his front room and whenever he has guests he shows them and says 'What do you think of my portrait, eh? What do you think of that?'

MARK. How long will it take Sarah to paint a lobster?

TONI. That's good…

MARK. Because it's best when they're fresh

TONI. Like how long is a piece of string

MARK. And if we had them tonight we'd just have herb butter and lemon

TONI. Except how long does it take to paint a lobster

MARK. But if we're going to freeze them then I'll make a bisque

GEORGE. I don't like bisque

MARK. You shouldn't eat seafood when you're /

GEORGE. Fuck off.

Pause. MARK *chops*.

FRED. When she's ready to mate, a female lobster has to shed her shell…

TONI (*touched*). Ohhh…

FRED. Leaving her entirely vulnerable.

TONI. Oh.

FRED. She needs to find a male for protection but the males don't like to share their dens, so the female has to seduce them.

TONI. How?

FRED. They piss in the dens.

GEORGE (*laughs gleefully*).

MARK. I don't see why that's / funny

TONI. She'll be a lobster! She'll be a lobster and she'll piss in all the dens! She'll piss in all the dens but she won't shed her shell. She'll just piss in the dens and run away.

MARK. Why are you so sure it's a girl?

TONI. What else would it be?

MARK. …

GEORGE *and* FRED *laugh.* TONI *too.*

Now I really don't see what's so funny…

GEORGE. No, you don't.

Bells out at sea.

FRED. Best be getting on…

GEORGE. You have to tell us a story before you go.

FRED. I've stayed too long already

TONI. We'll give you a shell in return.

FRED. Well in that case…

TONI. George, choose a shell.

GEORGE (*getting up*). What kind of shell do you want?

TONI. George is best at choosing shells

FRED. One for luck

TONI. It's a precise science.

MARK. …

GEORGE *considers the shells, then chooses one and brings it to* FRED.

GEORGE (*holding it out*). How's this?

FRED. Very nice /

GEORGE (*snapping it away*). Story first.

FRED (*after quite some thought*). A long time ago, around these parts, there was a young woman who was all set to marry the man of her parents' choice. The day before the wedding this young woman walked along the beach and she came across a man she'd never seen, sat on the shore, barefoot, and not a single possession save the clothes on his back to say where he'd come from and where he intended to go. Whether he was just a drifter passing through, or whether he'd drifted in from the sea Herself, she never knew, but he had a beautiful singing voice, and eyes like a rain sky when there's no telling where it meets the sea... So she liked him well enough, and was ruined. The next day, not a trace of the man, just as though he had never been, and her betrothed wouldn't have her after that and neither would her parents, and she swore the drifter would come back to her and she waited on the shore day and night, night and day, but he never did... So she cursed him, and all faithless men, and all sea creatures for good measure and to pay for her curse she cut out her heart and cast it into the waves, because the sea always has Her price. Now a sadness like that has its own way of living, and even without her heart, which by that time was as unnecessary to her as any warm feeling, the young woman didn't die, and she waits alone on the shore to this day. So if you see footsteps in the sand with no track as to where they came from, you'll know she's close, and you should pass on respectfully. And if you find on the shore, cast up by the tide, a strange object, black and soft as very old driftwood, and a shape to make you think of a human heart, you leave that where it lies. Because it belongs to the sea, and if you take it with you you'll only have sorrow to speak to...

GEORGE *gives him the shell.*

GEORGE. Thank you.

FRED. Thank *you.*

TONI. It was a good story

GEORGE. Nicely ambiguous

MARK. It's not ambiguous at all. It's a moral tale firmly set within a patriarchal tradition. I'm shocked you like it.

FRED. Who are you anyway?

MARK. ...

TONI. He's Mark. Robin's Mark.

FRED. Robin's here?

TONI. ...

MARK. ...

GEORGE. ...

FRED. ...

TONI. She's coming, she's just been delayed.

FRED (*leaving*). You'll give her my love when she gets here...

TONI. We will. Bye Fred.

FRED. Bye now.

TONI. Don't fall in.

FRED. I certainly won't.

GEORGE (*with him*). Are you going north or south?

FRED. North...

They go out by the sea door.

TONI. Fred has been telling us stories since I was little and we first came here. Every time he takes longer to start because he has to go through all the stories he knows and remember which ones he's already told us. One day I think he won't be able to find one and we'll just sit here in silence...

MARK. What is it, with the stories?

TONI (*after some thought*). I guess if we don't like them they don't have to be true.

MARK. Tell me a story then

TONI. Okay

MARK. A particular story

TONI. Which one

MARK. Where's Robin?

TONI. …

MARK. Where's Robin?

TONI. …

MARK. Where's Robin?

TONI. Some things…

MARK. …

TONI. Some things. I can't.

7. No Talking

Late evening.

They are all playing charades. GEORGE *is doing* The End of the Affair. *She keeps pointing at her belly and is getting more and more frustrated.*

TONI. Baby

SARAH. Belly?

TONI. Baby

SARAH. Stomach

SHIRLEY. Hand gestures

SARAH. Pregnant?

TONI. Embryo

SARAH. Pregnancy

TONI. Fetus

SHIRLEY. Waving your hands

SARAH. Shirley stop it

TONI. It's definitely baby

SARAH. *The Story of the Avocado Baby*?

SHIRLEY. That's six words

SARAH. Oh

TONI. *I Liked the Avocado Baby*

SHIRLEY. And the title is wrong

TONI. *I Liked the Avocado*

SARAH. I thought she might have misremembered

SHIRLEY. She wouldn't misremember

TONI. Baby

SHIRLEY. Frantic hand gestures

SARAH. Stop it Shirley! You're annoying her

SHIRLEY. Annoyance frustration *The Frustration of the Charader*

GEORGE. Fuck's sake!

TONI (*at once*). No talking no talking no talking!

SARAH (*at once*). Okay start again start again… (*Beat.*) Book. Five / words

SHIRLEY. And film.

SARAH. She didn't say film.

SHIRLEY. She did the first time.

SARAH. Is it? Fine. Book and film. Five words. First word

TONI. The

SARAH. Third word

TONI. Of

SARAH. Fourth word

SARAH/TONI. The…

SARAH. All together…

   GEORGE *gestures at her belly.*

TONI. Baby.

   GEORGE *smacks her palms into her face.*

MARK. *The End of the Affair.*

   Silence.

8. Other Mothers

Twilight. Duskly dark.

GEORGE *and* SARAH *drinking wine at the kitchen table.*

GEORGE. Sometimes I'd burn countries… If Spain were a threat to her I'd burn Spain. I'd burn anywhere. I'm not just talking about land mass.

SARAH. …

GEORGE. Other times… I think I want to kill her. In fact I think that's what I'm doing…

SARAH. These feelings might not be abnormal.

GEORGE. Well it shouldn't be normal

SARAH. You should speak to some other

GEORGE. It shouldn't be

SARAH. Other mothers.

GEORGE. …

SARAH. There are groups… (*Beat.*) You could speak to Shirley?

GEORGE. …

   They laugh.

SARAH. Yes…

> *A ship's horn out at sea.* SARAH *goes over to the glass and looks out.*

> Toni's still in the studio…

GEORGE. She's upset.

SARAH. Yes

GEORGE. It upsets her when he doesn't get out of bed

SARAH. Yes

GEORGE. And then tomorrow he'll get up and tell Toni off for not being dressed. But it's hypocritical.

SARAH. He's heartbroken…

GEORGE. Aren't we all.

SARAH. It takes patience. And a gentle hand… (*Pause.*) When I look out and see the studio windows lit up in the dark I feel safe. Do you feel safe when I'm in there and you see the lights?

GEORGE. Yes.

SARAH. I'm trying to do that with the painting. But it doesn't look safe, it looks lonely… I'm a little worried Toni is savaging it.

GEORGE. So you don't go too far out?

SARAH. Mm.

GEORGE. Would you like me to go and tell her off?

SARAH. No. Don't do that.

> SARAH *comes back to the table and pours them more wine.*

GEORGE. When we were little Shirley would go back to the university and leave us here… Toni remembers it goldenly. And it's true, we never wore shoes or brushed our teeth. We went swimming every day without suncream. We ate a whole tin of golden syrup once and were sick all night. It was heaven. At the same time I was the eldest and I had to tell them what to do…

SARAH. …

GEORGE. One night a man came into the house. We hid under my bed but I was ready to bite chunks out of his face. His shoes came into the bedroom and walked around. Robin and Toni were the smallest things in the world. We stayed under the bed till the sun came up. Later we looked around the house and he hadn't taken anything. But he'd left a shit in the toilet, a big stinking adult-man shit. Robin screamed and screamed. I sent them to hide in the shed and I cleaned the toilet until it was sparkling and the man had never been. I was thirteen years old… (*Pause.*) Help me.

SARAH. Oh… I don't know if I can…

GEORGE. Please…

SARAH. But I never wanted them… My ex did. And I pretended it wasn't happening and she became smaller and smaller and then she was gone

GEORGE. I like it when you talk about yourself

SARAH. I was so angry…

GEORGE. You turned up and started looking after us like it was normal but you're so contained

SARAH. I was angry for years. She loved an imaginary child more than she loved me. But now here I am with three daughters… (*Laughs.*) And recently I've found myself thinking about marriage!

GEORGE. Toni would love a wedding. You could always get divorced afterwards.

SARAH. Maybe it's just for the photograph. Just to say 'I was there with you' before she goes altogether where I can't follow…

SHIRLEY *comes in from the house*.

SHIRLEY. You're here… Hello.

SARAH/GEORGE. …

SHIRLEY. Today I was struck by a sense of not having my movements around the house followed. I'm developing a new thesis: there's no difference in essence between absence and presence. (*Beat*.) Did he go home?

SARAH. He didn't get out of bed.

SHIRLEY. Really?

SARAH. It's the second time.

SHIRLEY. Maybe he isn't angry. Maybe he's sad. But he's young so he doesn't know the difference… I think we should all be very nice to him.

SARAH. We are being nice to him Shirley.

GEORGE. I'm not.

SARAH. Are you going for your walk?

SHIRLEY. Yes.

SARAH. Will you check on the studio and see if Toni's taken a palette knife to my painting?

SHIRLEY. Yes.

She goes.

SARAH. Shirley?

SHIRLEY. …

SARAH. Don't go too far.

Beat.

SHIRLEY. Will you stay with me tonight?

SARAH. Yes.

SHIRLEY *goes out by the sea door.* GEORGE *rolls and lights a cigarette.*

I'm angry at her but I still want to be close…

GEORGE. You should leave us.

I wouldn't blame you.

SARAH. Where would I go? (*Pause*.) And you're asking me for advice? No… Sometimes it's good to sit together, and drink nice wine, and be normal for a little while before we sleep.

TONI *comes in by the sea door. Crying.*

TONI. I'm sorry… I got scared… I'm sorry I'm sorry…

SARAH *opens her arms and* TONI *runs over and is held and kissed and rocked.* GEORGE *smokes.*

SARAH. Never mind never mind… Ah well… Never mind…

9. To the Sea

Late afternoon. An unnatural dark. Thick clouds and wind stirring dangerously. Bells frantic out at sea.

MARK *and* TONI *at the glass.*

Lightning.

TONI. There!

MARK. Wait…

Pause.

Thunder, a low long growl.

There…

TONI. We're going to miss it…

They wait. More lightning, then thunder, a clap.

(*Calling.*) It's here! Hurry up!

GEORGE (*off, shouting*). I'm coming!

A deep breath.

The rain comes fierce and like a sigh.

Lightning and thunder, together.

TONI. Let's go!

She runs to the sea door.

MARK (*calling*). We're going!

GEORGE (*off, then entering, hurrying*). I'm carrying around a giant parasite you know!

MARK. Come on come on!

He takes her hand and they run out by the sea door with TONI *and down the garden path.*

SARAH (*off*). Where are you going!

TONI (*off*). To the sea!

SARAH (*off*). But the lightning!

MARK (*off*). Come with us!

Lightning and thunder.

SARAH *howls.*

GEORGE (*off*). Yes Sarah!

They are all gone to the sea. Their whoops and screams go with them. The storm happens in the kitchen.

Time passes.

SHIRLEY *comes in and makes a cup of tea and goes out again with the tea.*

Just the storm.

10. The Last Man

Midnight.

SARAH, TONI, GEORGE *and* MARK *at the table. Candles.*
They are all very drunk and have been for some time.

Pause.

GEORGE. No…

No I don't think I ever thought that…

MARK. No?

GEORGE. I don't think that was the thought that I…

Toni?

Beat.

TONI. Yes.

Beat.

MARK (*agreeing*). Yes…

GEORGE. Really?

SARAH. …

MARK. Umm…

Silence.

SARAH. I'm. So. Drunk… (*Beat.*) Can I have a cigarette…
George…

GEORGE *rolls and lights cigarettes for herself and* SARAH.

MARK. I really thought she was going to come…

TONI. She might still come

MARK. She said, there's a place where the shells go

TONI. She might

MARK. There's a studio at the bottom of the garden, it used to
be a shed, there are ghosts that we have to keep out

TONI. Grandpa

MARK. There's a gate that leads down to the sea

GEORGE. And other ghosts.

TONI. Grandpa was a fisherman, like Fred

GEORGE. Not like Fred

TONI. Grandpa was a fisherman but not like Fred

GEORGE. Grandpa used to shout at natural phenomena

TONI. Wind and rain and waves and things

GEORGE. And then once they'd ignored him completely he'd go and sit in the shed and cry

TONI. This was after Grandma had gone to the drowned village

GEORGE. She heard the bells ringing

TONI. There was no saving her...

GEORGE. Shirley was only little and she had to live with this shouting crying man for years and years

TONI. Until she escaped and ran away to the university to try and understand the meaning of life

MARK. That's not what she writes about...

TONI. And they never saw each other again

MARK. That's not

TONI. Because he wouldn't have her back

GEORGE. Even though he couldn't let her go

TONI. He cried all alone in the dark and then he died...

GEORGE. Before Sarah turned the shed into a studio you could still hear him crying when the wind came from the sea

TONI. Sometimes he still tries to get in because he's lonely

GEORGE. But we built strong walls and he can't get in...

TONI. Grandpa was the last man...

Pause.

MARK. My dad used to shout at things too… I promised myself I'd never shout at anything. And now I think I have all this shouting waiting to be shouted and I don't know how to keep it. In… (*Pause.*) Once. He shouted at a bicycle pump… And then. He tried to strangle the bicycle pump… And then he cried because it wouldn't die…

Beat.

They laugh. They laugh until they cry.

It dies.

A ship's horn out at sea.

Do you get scared?

At night?

GEORGE. Do you?

Silence.

MARK. What was Robin like… before?

TONI. Ohh she was. Perfect.

GEORGE. Toni hero-worshipped her

TONI. When she came into a room everyone smiled

GEORGE. Heroine-worshipped

TONI. And she was beautiful… She isn't really beautiful any more

MARK. She is

TONI. Because the things happened that you can't iron out…

MARK. I think she's beautiful

SARAH. …

TONI. After that, when she came into a room she sucked all the air into the corner where she was

GEORGE. Nobody smiled any more

MARK. I do

TONI. And she became harder and harder and then the cracks appeared

MARK. I smile...

TONI. And finally she crumbled away and when she was just a puddle of dust on the floor someone left a door open unthinkingly and there was a draft and she blew away...

GEORGE. Poof...

TONI. There was no saving her...

GEORGE. It was after that that Shirley stopped being able to distinguish between things altogether

TONI. And she never wrote again

GEORGE. The end.

SARAH (*deliberately and slowly, the most drunk, but quietly so*). I think it's disturbing that you think Robin is beautiful.

GEORGE *pours more whisky.*

MARK. I think it's disturbing that you let George smoke and drink when she's pregnant.

THE WOMEN (*slow and not unkindly*). Fuck off...

MARK. The baby will be damaged and you'll have to live with it and you'll be sorry...

GEORGE. I'll have to live with it anyway... And I'll be sorry. Anyway. (*Pause.*) I wanted to have a child because I needed to prove it was possible to be a mother... By the time I realised that it is not. Possible. It was too late to have an abortion... (*Cries.*) It's just that I'm pregnant. All. The time... (*Stops crying.*)

TONI. She'll be a damaged person. She'll be a damaged person and she'll never forgive us. And we'll never forgive Shirley. And Shirley will never forgive Grandpa. And Grandpa will never forgive the sea because he paid the price with Grandma but the sea cheated him and stopped giving him the fish

MARK. How long have I been here?

A ship's horn which turns out not to be a ship's horn but a low moan which breaks into a short sharp scream and is cut off.

MARK *leaps up*. THE WOMEN *don't respond*.

(*Terrified*.) What was that? What

GEORGE. Shirley has bad dreams...

MARK *standing, stricken*.

TONI. What's wrong?

Mark?

GEORGE. He's scared... (*Laughs*.)

MARK. I'm not scared

GEORGE. You are scared

MARK. I'm not

TONI. You're really scared! (*Laughs*.)

MARK. I thought someone had broken in

TONI (*giggling*). Broken in?

THE WOMEN *dissolve*.

MARK. Don't laugh at me! What am I supposed to do if someone breaks in all alone out here with two old ladies a pregnant woman and a demented girl /

TONI (*giggles*). Demented...

SARAH. I'm not old...

MARK. You don't know what it's like

TONI. Demented that's good

MARK. You don't know what it's like when the men come

TONI. When the...?

MARK. When she brings the men home

GEORGE. No

MARK. Or they come anyway and bang on the door

GEORGE. Stop

MARK. And I said you don't have to you don't

GEORGE. Stop you can't say it

MARK. And stand at the door with a knife because you don't know what they'll do when they come

GEORGE (*covering* TONI*'s ears*). Don't listen don't listen

MARK. And started to vanish when I wouldn't let her bring them home

TONI (*very still*). I'm not listening I'm not listening I'm not listening I'm not listening (*Continues and becomes a whisper.*)

MARK. Vanished for a day at first then for days then weeks so I said bring them back if you have to bring them back but please stay with me just stay with me because it's better that you're with me it's better that you're with me (*Puts his head in his hands and cries.*) Because I love you so... (*And cries.*)

GEORGE *takes her hands, cautious, away from* TONI*'s ears.*

TONI (*soft*). I'm not listening I'm not listening I'm not listening... I'm not...

Pause. They watch him cry.

Don't cry Mark...

GEORGE. Don't cry. Please don't cry...

TONI. We didn't know you could cry

GEORGE. We wouldn't have laughed if we'd known

TONI. We're sorry we're sorry...

They all sit miserably. TONI *dips her fingers in the candle wax, making wax caps for her fingers.* SARAH *tries to roll one of* GEORGE*'s cigarettes but is too drunk and makes a mess of it. She tries a few times.*

SARAH. It has, yes, since you've been wondering, occurred to me, not just once or twice but on several occasions over the years, that where Shirley is concerned, I may as well be… a dog. That she may as well be fucking, I won't say loving, a dog. (*Pause*.) That was crude. I didn't mean it like that… What I mean is that she doesn't distinguish between me and anyone else. Between me and any-*thing* else, even. And I may as well be… a refrigerator. Or a… spindle.

TONI (*trying it out*). Spinnn duhl…

SARAH. And if I were to give you a piece of advice, it would be to ensure that the person you love distinguishes between you and. Others… Because we should be distinguished. In our beloved's eyes… (*Gives up on the cigarette*.) *If I were to advise you further…* I would say… that you should ensure that your beloved has not made it their life's work to demonstrate that there is no difference between animate and inanimate objects, and to have done so so successfully that /

SHIRLEY (*off, plaintive*). Sarah…

Pause.

SARAH. You have to learn to live beside it. You have to learn to live with loss.

Beat.

GEORGE. I'll go. (*Going into the house*.) Everyone's crying tonight…

TONI (*touching* MARK*'s face with her wax caps*). This is how Robin feels. How she feels things.

SARAH. They're not listening anyway…

TONI. There's a skin between her and… everything else

SARAH. Nobody knows and nobody cares

TONI. She told me. She said, 'There's a skin between me and everything.'

SARAH. Nobody cares anyway…

TONI. It's a thin skin, but she may as well be /

MARK. Don't say it.

Beat.

TONI. Did you try to feed her the way you feed us?

MARK. …

TONI. We tried to feed her too. We thought if we fed her she wouldn't vanish into dust and blow away. But we were / wrong

MARK. Do you have a boyfriend?

TONI. …No.

MARK. A girlfriend?

TONI. No.

MARK. Have you ever even kissed someone?

TONI (*after some thought*). No.

MARK (*laughs*).

TONI. But I have had sex.

MARK. …

SARAH. Maybe I am old… Maybe I didn't even realise…

MARK. I think we should have sex.

TONI. What good would it do?

MARK. Seeing as no one distinguishes between anything around here

TONI. That's just Shirley

MARK. You're scared

TONI. No

MARK. You're scared of having sex

TONI. No

MARK. But you may as well be frying an egg

TONI. No

MARK. Or gutting a fish

TONI. No

SARAH. Maybe all the years passed and I didn't even notice...

MARK. You know what I hate most about you?

TONI. What?

MARK. Your conscious naivety.

TONI. What do you like most?

Beat.

MARK. Your conscious naivety.

TONI. You know what I like most about you?

MARK. ...

TONI. You love Robin.

You don't really know how, and you don't understand a lot of things, but really you /

MARK *lifts and shows* TONI *his hand. She goes still.*

MARK. You're taut as a bow string. A rabbit, or a deer, interrupted.

And you want to tell me how to love?

Beat.

SARAH. Just. Carelessness...

GEORGE *comes in.*

GEORGE. She's asleep.

Did he stop crying? Mark did you stop?

You did. Good...

It will get better.

Mark

MARK. Yes

GEORGE. It will get easier. I swear.

11. Help

Sunrise.

TONI *and* MARK. *They have sat up all night alone together. The candles have burned down.*

Birds, singing.

TONI (*eventually*). We could have sex. If you wanted.

I mean if you think it would help...

A loud crack.

Another.

And two and three

dozens of birds fly into the windows and crumple. Little sprays of blood on the glass, flutter of many surviving wings.

MARK *and* TONI *cling to each other.*

We could have sex. If you wanted.

I mean if you think it would help...

Beat.

MARK. Go to bed. Toni...

I'm so sorry.

Go to bed.

Birds, singing.

12. Under the Surface

Midday.

MARK *and an* OLD WOMAN. *She has just come in by the sea door. They stare at each other.*

MARK. Can I help you…?

OLD WOMAN. I'm looking for my skin.

MARK. …Excuse me?

OLD WOMAN. I'm looking for my skin. Do you know where it is? Will you help me find it?

MARK. Your

OLD WOMAN. Skin. I've been looking for years and years. He took it from me I never found it.

Beat.

MARK. Are you okay?

OLD WOMAN. I was. I was in the sea years and years ago when I was just a little thing rolled in the dark and the cool and up to the surface now just for the air and the foam how it gets you or maybe a fish delicious and flicker in the swell The foam's a horse you know a horse on the tide and the wind its driver beware an angry driver the horse whipped and beaten will dash its fury to dust on the rocks best dive deep down where it's still now and cool in the swirling and dark but if the driver's pleasant you can play in the rolling and tumbling all the sunshine hours just note how it gets you and don't mistake anger for play as any mammy will tell her calf So happy years many with my sisters and brothers and the salt on our whiskers and our grandam the moon to rustle and murmur our lullaby in light but a man sang to me from the rocks one night they always say beware a man singing don't trust his voice as far as it can lull you but lulled I was and wandered my way shorewards into his arms He had arms bronze from the sun kissed and lean from the hauling and harvest of bodies and he had legs too good legs to cling me

with and big lips to kiss me with and big boots to kick me
with and he had a back patterned the way they are a man's
back you can tell a man's anger from the look of his back
and look I did and thought I'd never seen anything so lovely
in all my slippery sliding days So flip flop onto the rocks a
big wave to aid me he strokes me and strokes and sings as he
strokes me patient as night all night till he strokes my skin
right off lay it did a puddle on the shore oh so raw the girl
beneath I thought it would end me all that desire fool mad in
the face of it all that flesh Never so hot the fire in his hearth
that night he carried me back in his arms my legs too
gangling and flop still for walking and laid me down in the
glow of his bed the pleasure of it was something remarkable
no lapping of wave or tickle of weed had ever could ever I'll
say to this day match the delectable of lovers' skin Morning
wake up stretch the limbs so new to me my muscles wound
round twist and turn and joints stiff as coral snap How nice!
but hear the gulls call to me hear the sea roar for me there the
man laid out beside me sleep so sweet butter wouldn't melt
so steal a kiss I do Goodbye! and up I get myself to head
back sea way tell my siblings all my story how wide their
eyes would prideful and delightful as I was But where's my
skin oh where's my skin where did I leave it down by the
shore must be all night no matter my brothers and sisters
would take good care and nuzzle it sandwards should the tide
greedy steal it out for we've a skill with things that float you
wouldn't believe Down to the shore naked as the night
before I was born run gaily and quick but a fear in my heart
pierced like a fish snapped up gulped by a sea bird rightly so
no skin on the shore or the rocks no skin in the rock pools
frantic and wandering up and down wailing He took it he hid
it He knew what he was about and without I'll never get
back to the sea no gill fish me or blow spout for gasping
before the long deep dive just limbs and hair and a face
wrought in sadness teeth always a little too sharp to be
natural but beauty more beautiful than any Man girl oh yes
he knew what he was about Out in the shallows my brothers
and sisters swelling and sobbing Gone gone Gone forever
nuzzle and nip at my finger hands nose and lick at my thighs
split so strange too late too late sink back down where never

I'll go again and slip through the cracks of all lost loved
things Lived with the man no choice that I had carried and
bore him in agony three calfs cut the rope himself he did
with his knife for the gutting and seal fat slitting and threw
the sea creatures all three on the embers curl black sea horse
steam spray rise up from the hearth spit and salt and hiss
before I'd even licked the film from their eyes and beat me
he did each time for a witch So that was life with the
cooking and the cleaning and the washing and fucking and
the carrying and the bearing and killing and the crying
cooking cleaning washing fucking carrying bearing killing
crying till one day a gannet pecked out his eyes just for a
laugh and serve him right But no matter my wheedlings and
sweetlings the years we've a way with words you wouldn't
believe he never did slip where he'd hid my skin so now
always caught between land and sea and sorrow my element
to swim in for as any mammy will tell her calf with no port
for returning you'll never know fair winds.

MARK. ...

OLD WOMAN. Have you seen my skin? If you help me find
my skin I'll give you your heart's desire.

SHIRLEY *comes in and makes a cheese sandwich and eats
it at the kitchen counter.*

MARK. I don't know where Robin is.

OLD WOMAN (*after some thought*). Is she in the sea? If she's
in the sea I'll find her there's not a nook cranny nor crevice
she can hide from me but I'll need my skin for that.

MARK. If you find Robin I'll help you find your skin

OLD WOMAN. She's not a mermaid is she? When they're
tadpoles they'll pull your whiskers and you'll never catch
them without a net, just look a fool in the attempt.

MARK. I don't think she's a mermaid...

OLD WOMAN. A mermaid's a silly thing till she's old but once
she's old she's wise as dying and cruel to match it, will drag
a man right down just for the pleasure of his struggle and the
feast.

MARK. She might be a mermaid...

OLD WOMAN. Best catch 'em while they're young and slit their pretty red tails in two and have your way, least that's what the harvesters on the boats say. No, I don't like mermaids...

Beat.

MARK. Why is there so much damage?

OLD WOMAN (*after some thought*). That's just how it is. Under the surface.

MARK. ...

OLD WOMAN. ...

The OLD WOMAN *leaves by the sea door.* SHIRLEY *eats her sandwich.*

Pause.

MARK. Was there an old woman here just now?

SHIRLEY. Yes, she was here. I'm surprised you didn't call the police.

MARK. The police?

SHIRLEY. She might have wandered off from a home somewhere. They do do that you know.

MARK. Why didn't you call the police?

SHIRLEY *holds up her sandwich.*

SHIRLEY. Maybe they'll find her before she / gets hurt...

MARK *runs out by the sea door.*

SHIRLEY *eats her sandwich.*

After a while MARK *comes in again slowly and stands very still in the middle of the room.*

SHIRLEY *eats her sandwich.*

13. Did You Shut the Drawer at Night?

Early evening.

They are finishing Sunday lunch outside, sat round the garden table. The kitchen is empty save the light and the sky and the sea.

SHIRLEY. And so I put her in a drawer

MARK. A drawer!

SHIRLEY. Well I had no money, no money for a cot

MARK. An actual drawer?

SHIRLEY. I pulled it out, not so far it could fall, and filled it with blankets and that's where she nestled.

GEORGE. Which explains everything I guess…

SHIRLEY. She was so little, I couldn't believe she was real…

GEORGE. I am real

MARK. But your parents didn't help?

SHIRLEY. My father never even knew he had granddaughters.

SARAH. It was better that way.

SHIRLEY. I heard from him one last time, after he died.
I received a letter, he'd left me the cottage… But he didn't have anything anyway, once the fish stopped coming to him…

A lobster comes in by the sea door, scuttles across the kitchen and into the house.

MARK. What did you do? With a PhD and a baby in a drawer?

SHIRLEY. The university gave me a room. And the head of the faculty gave her a velveteen rabbit

GEORGE. Ohh… my velveteen rabbit…

SHIRLEY. He was a very bitter man, hated everyone, hated everything, and he knocked on the door and when I opened it he thrust it at me and said / 'A rabbit for the cub…'

GEORGE/TONI. 'A rabbit for the cub!'

SHIRLEY. And he wouldn't hold you, wouldn't come in. He gave me the rabbit and ran away...

GEORGE. Where did it go? My velveteen rabbit...

MARK. Did you shut the drawer at night?

GEORGE. Mark!

SHIRLEY. Of course not!... Only sometimes, when I had to concentrate...

GEORGE. Shirley!

Bells out at sea.

SHIRLEY. The letter informs me also that my daughter, Robin, has not settled, that her relationships with the staff /

SARAH (*gentle*). Shirley...

SHIRLEY. Are not conducive to a healthy environment, that she persistently tries to leave the hospital grounds. We should go and collect her and bring / her home

SARAH. Shirley.

SHIRLEY. Can we go tomorrow?

Beat.

SARAH. We already did Shirley. Don't you remember?

GEORGE. We went in the old red car

TONI. We sat in the back and Sarah sat in the front with you

GEORGE. Robin sang 'Mary, Mary, Quite Contrary' the whole way home

TONI. She was happy.

SHIRLEY. ...

GEORGE. Silver bells and cockle shells do you remember?

TONI. And pretty maids all in a row?

SARAH (*begging*). Shirley...

Pause.

SHIRLEY. They say it's about a brothel, but they'll say anything given the chance… Who wants fruit? Cheese and fruit?

MARK. Let me help

SHIRLEY (*standing*). Sunday is my day. If I didn't do the lunch on Sunday I'd stop existing altogether

SARAH. Because I'd murder her

SHIRLEY (*walking away*). Untethered entirely from practical matters, I'd dissolve in abstraction

SARAH. Go and get the fruit!

SHIRLEY. And scatter myself among the stars, heaven at last…

SHIRLEY *comes in by the sea door. She just sees the tail of the lobster scuttle into the house. After a moment's pause she goes to the counter and prepares the fruit and the cheese on a tray. Outside they speak soft.*

MARK. She should see a doctor.

GEORGE. 'A doctor.' (*Laughs.*)

MARK. I'm serious

TONI. You're always serious

MARK. It's going to get worse

TONI. I think you should invest in a little silliness

MARK. Aren't you worried?

TONI. Your portfolio should include…

GEORGE. Why should we be worried?

TONI. Clowning, practical jokes

MARK. It might be early-onset

TONI. Toilet humour

MARK. It might be early-onset dementia.

Several lobsters come in by the sea door and scuttle across the kitchen. SHIRLEY *turns with the tray, stops, and watches them.*

GEORGE. We can always bring her back

TONI. It's true, we can always bring her back

GEORGE. And besides, it's worse here. It'll be better when we're at the university.

MARK. You say it's better or worse so you know it's bad

TONI. Mark thinks it's important to pay respect to structural boundaries

MARK. I don't see

TONI. Such as time.

MARK. …

TONI. But Shirley stopped paying respect to structural boundaries. Shirley inhabits the liminal places

GEORGE. The shoreline, the surface

TONI. Someone has to, after all

MARK. It's impossible talking to you…

SHIRLEY *goes out the sea door with the tray.*

GEORGE. 'Impossible.' (*Laughs.*)

TONI (*laughing*). George we're impossible!

SHIRLEY (*appearing behind the glass*). The cottage was not built with a view to a view, that is, a sea view. You can't eat the scenery (*She puts the tray on the table.*) as my father used to say. Sarah, would you tell us what these are?

SARAH. Let's see… That one's a nice soft goat's cheese, from Wales

SHIRLEY. But you can eat what's in the scenery. So the cottage was built, by my great-grandfather, to be close to the scenery so as to harvest what was in it

SARAH. And this is a Strathdon Blue

SHIRLEY. The kitchen extension, on the other hand, which we have Sarah to thank for – thank you Sarah

SARAH. You're welcome

SHIRLEY. Was designed and built for the purpose of looking out at the sea…

SARAH. And this is a mild Irish sheep's cheese

SHIRLEY. Delicious.

Time passes as SHIRLEY *speaks. The kitchen is submerged in the sea, and the sea creatures inhabit where humans once were.*

What we didn't take into account is this means that the sea can look back in at us, has looked at us, and has made Her calculations… The water has been rising and falling, rising and falling for millions of years, and will continue to rise now for some thousands of years more, by which time this cottage, like those that came before it and settled too close to the harvest, will be long gone, reclaimed by the sea for the sea's own purpose…

The kitchen returns to the present.

Beat.

(*Thoughtful.*) Perhaps we can herd them out with brooms…

They pass and cut and eat the cheese and fruit.

MARK (*eventually*). And your mother?

SHIRLEY. Whose mother?

MARK. What happened to your mother?

Beat.

SHIRLEY. She used to leave me presents on the shore, lovely shells and sometimes fish… But then she started to forget. Or maybe I started to forget… It's dark down there. Best not to dive too deep…

14. Maybe He'll Get Septicaemia and Die

Late afternoon.

GEORGE *is taking a splinter out of* MARK*'s hand with a needle.* TONI *is watching. A colander of green beans on the table.*

Pause.

GEORGE. You're in my light. Toni.

   Pause.

TONI. There it is!

MARK. Ow.

GEORGE. Sorry

MARK. It's fine

GEORGE. It's quite deep...

MARK. Just go for it.

   Pause.

GEORGE. Toni you're in my light.

TONI. Poor wounded Mark. Maybe he'll get septicaemia. And die.

MARK. Shall I do it?

TONI. Yes, we knew a man called Mark once. He came to stay and was killed by a beanpole. The infection spread and there was nothing to be done.

   Pause.

MARK. Do you want me to do it?

GEORGE. I'm doing it

MARK. You're being too careful

GEORGE. I don't want to hurt you

MARK. I don't care if you hurt me.

GEORGE. ...

MARK. I want you to hurt me.

> **GEORGE** *looks at him, lays his hand flat and pushes the needle through slowly.*

> **Oh... Ah...** *Ah!*

TONI (*screams*)**. Stop it!**

MARK. You're being too careful

GEORGE. I don't want to hurt you

MARK. I don't care if you hurt me.

GEORGE. It takes patience. And a gentle hand...

> *Pause.*

MARK. If you'd just /

GEORGE. Goat's cheese and onion tart.

> *Beat.*

MARK. Goat's cheese and onion tart?

GEORGE. Can you make a goat's cheese and onion tart?

MARK. Easy.

GEORGE. And you make the pastry?

MARK. Of course.

> *Pause.*

GEORGE. Spaghetti alle vongole.

> *Beat.*

MARK. Yes.

> *Beat.*

TONI. Apple and celeriac bake.

MARK. Yes

GEORGE. Shepherd's pie.

MARK. Yes

TONI. Stargazy pie?

MARK. Oh yes.

GEORGE. Marzipan ice cream?

MARK. Any ice cream

TONI. Rhubarb fool?

MARK. Challenge me.

GEORGE. Ossobuco

MARK. Yup

TONI. Bouillabaisse

MARK. Yup

GEORGE. Saddle of rabbit of hare and of lamb

MARK. Yup yup yup

TONI. Is there anything you can't make?

MARK. When there isn't a recipe.

TONI. Like?

MARK. Robin come back. (*Silence*.) Sometimes. When we were at the hospital together. She would start dancing… She stretched her arms up to the ceiling, like she could reach through to the sky…

Pause.

GEORGE. You're in my light. Toni…

MARK. Ah…

GEORGE. There.

MARK. Thank you.

GEORGE *holds the splinter on her finger to his lips.*

GEORGE. Make a wish.

Beat.

He blows.

SARAH *comes in from the house with shopping bags. They stare at her.*

SARAH. It is the *strangest* thing going into town after you've been here for a while. Where do all these people come from? Now, if it's alright with our ambitious sous chef here, I picked up some tuna steaks and I thought we could make a Niçoise for supper.

MARK. The beans were getting wild on the trellis so I picked them

TONI *(pleased)*. Trellis...

SARAH. That's perfect then

GEORGE *(the baby)*. Fuck off!

MARK. What?

SARAH *is unpacking the bags.* MARK *and* TONI *are topping and tailing the beans at the table.*

TONI. It's the baby.

MARK. Oh. *(Pause.)* Maybe she wants to be born...

GEORGE. Don't...

MARK. So she can wander about in the world

GEORGE. It's terrible

MARK. See what it's like.

TONI. Maybe she'll be an explorer.

GEORGE. I hate explorers

MARK. And she'll explore the only places that are left to explore...

GEORGE. ...

TONI. ...

SARAH. ...

MARK. I mean the extremes and the edges of places...

TONI. She'll go to space and the bottom of the ocean

MARK. And she'll always know how to find her way back. She won't feel the cold or be afraid of the dark and no harm will come to her. The tides and the currents will be her friends, gravity will make an exception for her and the stars will take her by the hand...

They top and tail the beans.

15. Where Love Lies

Sunset.

TONI *and* MARK *at the table.* MARK *is reading a book very seriously. He has a pencil. Sometimes he makes a note in the book very seriously with the pencil.*

TONI (*eventually, singing*). 'Ohhhh ayeeeeee... Do like to be beside the seaside /'

MARK *glares at her. She stops. He goes back to his work.*

Pause.

'Ohh I do like to be /'

MARK *glares at her. She stops. He goes back to his work.*

'Beside the seeeeeeeeeeea /'

MARK *glares at her. She stops. He goes back to his work.*

Pause.

(*Quick.*) 'OhIdoliketobebesidetherumpumpum /'

MARK *glares at her. She stops. He goes back to his work.*

Beat.

(*Very soft and plummy.*) 'Where the brass band plays tiddly-om-pom /'

They leap up. MARK *chases her screaming round the table and out the sea door. They run backwards and forwards outside the glass and down into the garden.*

(*Off.*) Saaaaaaraaaahhhhh! Sarah Sarah Sarah Sarah (*etc.*)

SHIRLEY *comes into the kitchen, passes the book on the table. Stops. Looks at it. Reads standing.*

A leafy twiggy crash.

MARK, *off, yells.*

SHIRLEY *has picked up the pencil and is writing in the book.* MARK *comes in by the sea door. Watches her.*

MARK (*eventually*). What are you writing?

SHIRLEY. Of course you're there…

She goes back to writing, spinning the book round so she can write up the margin.

MARK. What are you writing?

SHIRLEY (*still writing*). Just a footnote.

MARK (*holding his hand out*). I broke a cuttlebone in the garden. I stepped on it. I'm sorry…

SHIRLEY. I read your PhD.

MARK. …

SHIRLEY (*stopping*). You write well, you reason well and, despite your pretence, you have an imagination, but… You come to the wrong conclusions.

Pause. SHIRLEY *writes.*

MARK. Were you disappointed in me?

SHIRLEY (*eventually*). There. Myself, at least, rescued from the murky depths of past / error

MARK. How long has it been since you've published?

Beat.

SHIRLEY. I expect you're going to tell me

MARK. Ten years.

SHIRLEY. ...

MARK. What do you know about the right or the wrong conclusions when you've made yourself irrelevant to the whole conversation?

SHIRLEY. Time moves fast now does it?

MARK. Are you working on something new?

SHIRLEY. ...

MARK. You are, aren't you?

SHIRLEY. No.

MARK. ...No?

SHIRLEY. No.

MARK. No...

What do you do in your study all day, if you're not writing?

SHIRLEY. I sleep.

MARK. That. Is appalling.

SHIRLEY. When you're older you'll know sleep is its own achievement.

MARK. That a third of my life will be spent wasting time asleep terrifies me.

SHIRLEY. The nights are hard for dreamers.

MARK. ...

SHIRLEY. Oh yes. I know.

Pause. SHIRLEY *reads*.

MARK. It's just that the sea is so loud sometimes it's like the tide's coming in under the bed.

SHIRLEY. ...

MARK. In the bad dreams she's already too far out and I'm waving from the shore...

In the good dreams... I'll never let her go. And we drown

SHIRLEY. How thick is your skin?

MARK. …

SHIRLEY. Thick, I hope, if you want to hold on to a vanishing object.

MARK. …

SHIRLEY. Soon there'll be nothing left and you'll be stuck fast with the effort, your arms sealed round an empty space… That's where love lies, in the longing for the absent thing, gloriously imagined, and gloriously remembered.

MARK. My mum left when I was two. My dad blamed me. He couldn't look at me. I've spent my life trying to make another family but I only know how to find barren ground.

SHIRLEY. Look at you… Exhausted from all your thrashing about. Best just get on with it… Salvage. *Salvage*. Salvage what you can from the wreck.

Pause. SHIRLEY *reads.*

MARK. She isn't going to come, is she?

SHIRLEY. …

MARK. She isn't going to come to me again, is she?

SHIRLEY. No. I think. Not… (*Closes the book, stands. Beat.*) You can stay here if you want.

MARK. Here?

SHIRLEY. This is a thin place. The girls built strong walls to make up for it but I find there's always a crack for the ghosts to get in. You wouldn't be lonely…

TONI *runs in by the sea door.*

Yes. Toni. Good…

SHIRLEY *goes out by the sea door.*

TONI. Sarah says she's going to start making dinner soon so I thought I'd tell you so you can get there first.

MARK. …

TONI. Not because you're better than her although secretly you are but really because I know you like to and I wanted to make up for disturbing you earlier.

MARK. …

TONI. So what's for dinner?

Mark? What's for dinner Mark?

I'll help if you promise not to show me how to chop things.

MARK. Have you ever made ravioli?

TONI. No!

MARK. Would you like to?

TONI. …

MARK. It involves kneading and rolling and cutting out little shapes with a sharp mould but no chopping.

TONI. Yes then.

MARK. Crab ravioli is for dinner.

TONI. And a bitter salad?

MARK. And a bitter salad.

They gather. GEORGE *comes in with the Jenga and empties it onto the table and plays a game of Jenga.*

Would you like to crack the eggs?

TONI. Yes.

MARK. First we have to separate a yolk. Cup your hands over the bowl… (*He cracks an egg into her hands.*) See how alive it is, how once-contained.

TONI. Yes.

MARK. Now let the white run through your fingers… Good… See what remains. A golden thing…

16. The Book of Revelation

Late evening.

They are playing charades. SHIRLEY *is doing* The Naked Lunch. *The choice of title is functional rather than significant.*

SARAH. Second word…

TONI. Skin. Skin?

GEORGE. Flesh

TONI. Flesh or skin

MARK. It's not skin

SARAH. Arm!

MARK. She'd say if it were skin

SARAH. Arm… femur…

TONI. Skin

MARK. Stop saying skin

SARAH. Is the femur in the arm?

TONI. Epidermis

MARK. Stop it

GEORGE. Maybe she's trying to show us how many syllables there are

SARAH. Are you trying to show us… No.

TONI. Tap… Percussion… Drum skin!

MARK. That's two words. And it's not skin

GEORGE. Well it's not like you're contributing anything

SARAH. Frustration

MARK. Because I'm thinking

SARAH. Frustrated gestures

GEORGE. That's a poor game plan

SARAH. Flapping about in frustration

GEORGE. You need to trigger ideas

MARK. No you need to focus

SARAH. Flappy flappy flappy flap

> SHIRLEY *puts her hands on her hips.*

> Ha! See what it's like?

TONI. I think it's skin.

> SHIRLEY *sighs and undresses.*

> *All at once:*

GEORGE (*laughs, gleefully*).

SARAH. Oh no Shirley no no no no no no no (*etc.*)

TONI (*points*). Skin! Skin skin skin skin skin skin skin (*etc.*)

MARK. Reveal! Revelation! The Book of Revelation! And a great mountain burning with fire was cast into the sea and the third part of the sea became blood; and the third part of the creatures which were in the sea died; and the third part of the ships were destroyed...

17. For the Journey

Late morning.

MARK, SARAH *and* FRED THE FISHERMAN. FRED *at the table, no lobsters, a mug of tea, an empty plate, crumbs of meringue.*

SARAH (*putting an envelope on the table*). This is money for the cleaner

MARK. …

SARAH. I've written her number on the envelope, you just call and let her know when you leave.

MARK. …

SARAH. And this is some money for you, for the / train

MARK. I don't want your money.

SARAH. …

MARK. I don't want you to go.

SARAH. Well… You stay as long as you like. Just post the keys through the letterbox.

MARK. When will you come back?

SARAH. Oh. Christmas I guess, at least all together.

MARK. What will you do if I'm still here at Christmas?

Beat.

SARAH. They'll keep you if you want.

If that's what you want.

Is that what you want?

Beat.

MARK. Why do you only paint lobsters?

Beat.

SARAH. I don't.

FRED (*laughs*).

SARAH. I have, in fact, as far as I can remember, never painted a lobster.

MARK. What do you paint?

SARAH. When I'm here I paint cityscapes. When I'm in the city I paint seascapes. So really what I'm doing is painting memories. Which is why Toni is scared that one day I won't find my way back.

MARK. Like Shirley?

Beat.

SARAH. Or Robin.

Car horn.

GEORGE (*off, faint*). Sarah!

SARAH. I have to go…

MARK. Will you.

Let me know if everything's okay. With George, at the hospital.

SARAH. I'm sure that can be arranged… Bye Fred. I'm sorry you came all this way on a leaving day.

FRED. It's happened before, it'll happen again.

SARAH *goes out through the house.*

FRED *and* MARK *listen to the car door slam, then the car engine start, then the car driving, then the car stopping, then a car door. Eventually* TONI, *dressed, runs in from the house.*

TONI. Sarah says you'll be here at Christmas.

MARK. I might be.

TONI. That's good. You can meet the baby.

MARK. If you come back before Christmas I can help you apply to university.

TONI. I don't want to go to university. I want to help look after the baby.

MARK. Looking after a baby is all very well but it isn't a sensible occupation for a demented girl.

TONI (*laughs*). Maybe she'll be a man. A sad angry man, but a nice man. Like you.

MARK. Maybe.

Car horn.

TONI. Bye Fred. Don't fall in.

FRED. I certainly won't.

TONI (*running out, calling*). See you at Christmas...

Car door, car engine, car driving, horn calling goodbye a few times, then the car gone.

FRED (*eventually*). I remember them when they were just little things... The three of them together, they'd squeeze into the smallest places and chatter to each other I don't know what... They were lovely. And wild. And very lonely.

MARK. Do you want another cup of tea?

FRED (*standing*). Best be getting on...

MARK. Don't you. Have to tell me a story before you go?

Beat.

FRED. What'll you give me in return?

*After some consideration, **MARK** takes out his heart and puts it on the table in front of **FRED**. It is a black, soft, sad thing. Like very old driftwood.*

(*Pocketing it.*) **That'll do...**

MARK. Don't you. Have to tell me a story before you go?

FRED. What'll you give me in return?

MARK. The last meringue? For the journey.

FRED. You don't want it?

MARK. I don't like sweet things. They were for Toni.

FRED. That'll do nicely then.

MARK *takes the plate of meringues to the counter and wraps the last one in a napkin.*

Let's see now... There was once a boy whose father was a fisherman, and his grandfather was a fisherman, and his father before him and his father before him, all the way back to when we first crawled out of the sea, and the sea, being proud, never let us come back, which is why all men are filled with a longing for the sea. And when this boy was still a boy his father took him out on the boat to haul up the traps, and the sea gave Herself up excessive that night, each trap stuffed full with harvest, and the boy's father was gleeful, which made him a fool, because a man should never trust a too-generous sea... The hours passed each one as like to the last, and the boy thought he'd go mad with it, the spray and the wind and the dark and the hauling, and the spray and the wind were one element and no different, and the click-clacking of the lobsters scheming in their traps, till the boy came at last to a trap that wouldn't come, and his father, even, couldn't raise it up, and only when they heaved both together did it surprisingly sudden come free... The boy saw first. And knew it was wrong. The dark shape quick in the black water, bigger so fast he thought it might never stop but engulf the whole sea, a hungry thing. Then the sea gave it up, as the sea is sometimes wont to do, and sometimes never, and the boy's father saw too and raised the alarm of a man overboard, but it wasn't a man, and in truth by then it wasn't even a woman. Just a swollen slippery memory of a thing once living, half-eaten carcass, nibbled and sucked at, and that explained the harvest, because a lobster will eat anything... Now some blame the father, for there are things a man does not know how to say to a boy, so they sailed home in silence and the boy learned the lesson of silence. And some say it was the sea, that She took his voice to pay for the harvest, because the sea always has Her price. Whichever it was one thing I know, and that is from that day to this the boy carries alone the dead thing with him, and from that day to this he has not said a single word...

MARK (*giving him the meringue*). Thank you.

FRED. Thank *you*. They're good meringues.

MARK. I whisked the egg whites myself.

FRED. It makes it better then?

MARK. Actually I just need to fill the hours. Repetitive gestures are good for focusing.

FRED. On what?

MARK. Anything but.

FRED (*laughs*).

MARK (*shy*). Will you come again?

FRED. If that's what you want…

   Pause.

MARK. Perhaps… It was Robin. The thing in the sea.

   Beat.

FRED. Could be…

   MARK *walks him to the sea door.*

MARK. Will you go north or south?

FRED (*off*) Oh south. South…

   FRED *is gone.*

   MARK *tidies up then goes into the house. Eventually he comes back again with a towel, in swimming trunks, and goes out by the sea door. Then it's just the kitchen, the glass, the sky, the light and the sea.*

SHIRLEY (*meanwhile*). Heard, last night, an echo with no source sound. Wondered if Robin had come at last and if she were calling me. Went down to the sea, the sea being the source of all things, but on the shore, a shock. Not Robin, but my father there. I knew him at once for his lantern, and how he railed at the sea in the night in his grief. But I wasn't afraid, I called out to him, 'Give up! Give up now and go

away! They'll never come back, they'll never come back,
they'll never come again...' Woke to the sea calm as a
mirror, cold, very cold, and very alone, and I know it's time
for us to go... As I wandered homeward bound, at the
horizon where sea meets sky and all around where sky meets
land... There... The dawn. A pale sun, rising.

End.

www.nickhernbooks.co.uk

facebook.com/nickhernbooks

twitter.com/nickhernbooks